CLEAR

THE
WAY

Printed in the United States of America

First Edition, 2026

E-book ISBN: 979-8-9942436-2-6
Paperback ISBN: 979-8-9942436-1-9
Hardback ISBN: 979-8-9942436-0-2

Book Design by Ian Koviak
www.bookdesigners.com

Copyediting by Liz Wheeler

DESIGNING MEETINGS WITH
PURPOSE, CLARITY, AND IMPACT

CLEAR
THE
WAY

Saving the World
One Meeting at a Time

KERRI SUTEY

CONTENTS

INTRODUCTION

Meetings were never meant to be the center of work. They began as places to gather, share information, make decisions, and coordinate across teams. Over time, they quietly multiplied. As organizations grew more complex and communication moved online, meetings became the default way to solve problems, share updates, or feel connected. The intention behind them faded; the habit remained.

Today, meetings shape how people experience their work more than almost any other structure. They influence how well teams collaborate, how decisions get made, how leaders communicate, and how cultures form. When meetings are strong, work feels clear and energizing. When they aren't, the effects ripple through slow decisions, misalignment, disengagement, and the sense of constantly being busy but rarely making progress.

Over the past twenty years, I have coached leaders and teams across multiple industries, from Google, IBM, Loyola University of Maryland, the US Department of Defense, and ExxonMobil, and the story is consistent. People are moving fast, working hard, and doing their best with the information they have. But meetings slow them down. They are tired of meetings that lack purpose, direction, and relevance to them. They're tired of spending their days in conversations that don't move anything forward. And they're tired of feeling their time is treated as an endless resource rather than a shared, finite asset.

This book is built on the belief that clear meetings create clear work, and clear work creates better results. Meetings don't have to feel heavy or complicated. They can be energizing and productive. They can be a place where people feel seen, respected, and aligned. They can be designed intentionally rather than inherited passively.

The CLEAR framework emerged from thousands of hours spent coaching leaders and teams through challenges, redesigning meeting habits, and watching what works in practice. But CLEAR didn't appear in isolation. Its roots go back to a simple, meaningful framework I learned from my teachers, originally created by Leslie Riley: The POWER Start. Leslie created POWER years ago, shared it generously with others, and modeled what intentional meeting design can make possible. CLEAR evolved from that foundation through lived experience, real-world application, and the needs of the leaders and teams I serve today. I'm deeply grateful for Leslie's creativity, generosity, and influence. CLEAR exists because POWER walked it first.

This book is a guide to designing meetings that create progress rather than drain energy. It's written for anyone who leads, attends, or shapes meetings of any kind: executives, managers, project leads, facilitators, coaches, educators, and cross-functional teams. You can read it cover to cover or open it whenever a meeting needs to be rethought. It's meant to be a useful resource, a guide.

If you've ever left a meeting thinking, "There has to be a better way," this book is your invitation to create that way. If you've ever wondered what your meetings say about your leadership, this book will help you answer that question with confidence and clarity.

Meetings will always be a part of work. But with intention and design, they can become one of the most powerful tools you have to build alignment, connection, and momentum.

Let's begin.

PART I

THE PROBLEM & THE PROMISE

An organization's culture is reflected in its meetings: when they happen, and what they're like. By rethinking how workers meet, it's possible to transform a lot more than just the meetings themselves.

CHAPTER 1

THE COST OF UNCLEAR MEETINGS
When clarity is missing, everything takes longer

We've all been there. You walk into the 9:00 a.m. meeting—whether into a conference room or onto a video call—coffee in hand, ready to get to work. A few people are whispering side conversations, someone is wrestling with their audio settings, another is speed-reading a deck they probably should have opened yesterday, and several others are sitting quietly, wearing the universal expression of "I have so much actual work to do today."

The host welcomes you, and the group settles into that quiet, predictable silence. At 9:04 a.m., the leader announces the most predictable sentence in modern work: "Let's wait a minute for a few more people." You glance at the invite and discover that, of course, there is no agenda.

The meeting kicks off with no clear direction: a small update, a side question, a low-stakes detail that does not deserve the screen time it's about to get. Ten minutes pass. Then twenty. You're still talking about the least important item because, well, it's the easiest one to tackle. The real priorities are sitting patiently in the corner, wondering if anyone remembers they exist.

What is striking is not the moment itself but how normal it is. It happens inside global corporations, nonprofits, universities, government agencies, and startups. Different languages. Different industries. Same experience. A meeting begins without real clarity, follows a loose path of updates, and ends an hour later, if it ends on time, with little to show for it.

People assume this is the cost of modern work. A necessary

inconvenience. Yet buried in that assumption is an unintended lesson: when meetings lack clarity, people learn to expect less from them. They show up prepared for disappointment rather than progress.

THE HIDDEN COST OF FRAGMENTATION

Research shows that employees spend close to three hours each week simply coordinating or rescheduling meetings, not including the time spent preparing for them. Studies also indicate that more than half of meetings interrupt focused work, making it harder for people to regain momentum afterward. The cost is not just time and money. It is momentum.

Research also shows that when meetings fill the day, people lose the uninterrupted focus time required for meaningful work. Even short meetings create fragmentation that makes simple tasks feel heavier and complex work nearly impossible to start. This constant context switching slows thinking, increases fatigue, and reduces the quality of decisions. And when meetings lack clarity, they don't just take more time than necessary; they impact the time between meetings that people spend on thinking, creating, and solving problems. A meeting that lacks clarity results in a poor understanding of the organization's goals, priorities, and timelines, which results in individual workers or teams that are less efficient.

Bad meetings are not simply annoying. They carry a cultural cost that organizations rarely see clearly. It shows up in the way people behave: cameras off, screens split between video, work, and emails, participation shrinking to a handful of voices. Decisions are deferred until "next time." Ideas remain unspoken because the purpose never felt grounded or participants didn't feel confident enough to contribute. Leaders walk out of one meeting only to walk into another. Over time, talking about the work replaces doing the work.

The cost of poor meetings shows up long before the quarterly results ever do. It appears in the moment someone logs in already tired, in the hesitation before unmuting, in the ideas held back because the room felt too crowded or the pace too rushed.

THE CULTURAL CONSEQUENCES

Look closely, and you will see that meetings sit at the center of many problems described by workers: misalignment, slow decisions, repeated conversations, and feeling stretched thin. Meetings are where priorities are shaped, relationships are built, and decisions are made. They are also where confusion spreads, where momentum is lost, and where culture reveals itself most honestly.

Meetings are not neutral moments. They are cultural mirrors. When meetings start late, the message is clear: workers' time isn't valued. When meetings run long, the message is clear: boundaries are optional. When meetings end without agreements, the message is clear: accountability is negotiable. And when meetings exist out of habit, but are unproductive, the message is clear: change is not valued.

These messages accumulate. People absorb them even when no one says them out loud. Over time, meetings shape the expectations, energy, and trust inside a team more than most leaders realize.

Research shows that poorly structured meetings also contribute to burnout. When people spend most of their day in conversations that lack direction or relevance, they leave meetings depleted instead of energized. The workload does not decrease, but the time available to complete it does. Even capable and motivated people begin to feel overwhelmed, not because they cannot do the work, but because the meeting culture works against their ability to do it well.

Organizations often try to solve meeting problems by focusing on the number or frequency of meetings. Meeting-free Fridays. Shortening the hour to forty-five minutes. But the problem is rarely the number. The deeper issue is that many meetings are launched without understanding why they exist or what they need to accomplish. In the absence of clarity, meetings do what they have always done. They drift.

THE WAY FORWARD

The trust cost of ineffective meetings is not measured only in money or hours. It is measured in missed opportunities for alignment, wasted cognitive energy, diluted trust, and slow progress toward the work that matters most. People do not want more time in their day. They want more impact in their day.

Here is the good news. The meeting culture you inherit does not have to be the meeting culture you keep. Meeting problems are solvable. They are solvable in every industry, every team size, every culture, and every organizational stage. When leaders design conversations with intention, they unlock something powerful. People feel seen. Decisions move faster. Ownership becomes clearer. Meetings begin to energize rather than deplete.

Better meetings are not created by chance. They are created by choice. That choice begins by noticing the real cost of the meetings we tolerate. Once you see it, you cannot unsee it. And once you see it, you can begin to change it.

In the next chapter, we'll dive a bit deeper into the importance of creating a culture of clear communication. In Part II, I'll show you how to bring clarity to life, one CLEAR meeting at a time.

CHAPTER 1 REFLECTION

Use these questions to deepen your thinking before you move on:

- What meeting patterns have I tolerated that may be slowing my team down more than I realized?

- Which meetings leave me feeling energized, and which leave me feeling depleted? What explains the difference?

- How do my meetings signal what my team values or neglects?

- If I redesigned one recurring meeting from the ground up, what would I remove, add, or completely reimagine?

CHAPTER 2

WHY CLARITY MATTERS
Clarity fuels progress

During my time as chief of staff in a global marketing organization, we were navigating two major transitions at once: returning to the office and adopting agile ways of working. Teams were tired. Leaders were stretched. Priorities shifted weekly. In one leadership meeting, we spent over an hour debating which initiatives were "top priority," only to realize we were using the same word to describe entirely different things.

We weren't misaligned because we disagreed. We were misaligned because we had made assumptions, rather than being clear. When we finally paused to define what we meant by "priority," the conversation shifted. Topics that felt tense softened. People stopped talking past one another. Decisions that once felt impossible suddenly moved forward with ease. What changed wasn't the work. It was the clarity.

That moment taught me something many leaders discover the hard way: clarity accelerates everything it touches. When people understand what matters, why it matters, and how to contribute, they stop second-guessing and start moving forward with confidence.

WHY CLARITY MATTERS MORE THAN EVER

Today's organizations operate in a landscape that is more complex, distributed, and interdependent than anything we've experienced before. Teams collaborate across time zones, tools, and functions. Hybrid work reduces casual alignment and increases the potential for assumptions.

Clarity reduces that friction. It lowers cognitive load, reduces rework, speeds up decision-making, and makes collaboration easier. Without clarity, people waste energy interpreting rather than contributing. With clarity, they can use their energy to get the work done.

Research shows that constant meetings reduce the amount of uninterrupted focus time people have each day, which makes even simple work feel heavier. When teams protect focused work by being intentional about meetings, overall performance rises.

Studies have also found that employees often leave meetings unclear about what was accomplished or how decisions were made, which slows progress and creates rework. When you consider how many work processes rely on meetings for alignment, the cost of unclear expectations becomes unmistakable.

Across multiple studies, a consistent message emerges: unclear meetings weaken the systems organizations rely on. They reduce focus time, multiply unnecessary coordination, slow decision-making, and contribute to burnout. But when meetings are designed with clarity, the opposite becomes true. Workflows stabilize. Cognitive load decreases. Teams feel more aligned and less exhausted. Clear meetings do more than fix a calendar problem. They strengthen the cultural patterns that determine how work actually gets done.

Clarity is not a luxury. It is a leadership behavior with cultural consequences.

THE BLIND SPOT IN COMMUNICATION

Many leaders believe they are being clear when they are not. Not because they lack skill, but because clarity in their head feels like clarity in the room. This creates a few predictable blind spots.

People assume others share their mental model. They rarely do. Leaders think they communicate more than they actually do.

Teams believe they understand the goal until the moment they begin, and misalignment surfaces. Leaders underestimate how much cognitive energy ambiguity requires. They feel the pressure of speed, while their teams feel the pressure of uncertainty.

THE RIPPLE EFFECT OF CLEAR MEETINGS

Clear meetings make both meetings and work better. When meetings begin with a clear purpose and defined outcomes, people arrive more prepared. When the right voices are present, decisions become more informed. When roles and expectations are explicit, contributions become balanced and new ideas become possible. People engage with commitment rather than compliance when they understand how the meeting is relevant to their work.

Clarity creates room for creativity, confidence, and psychological safety. Teams that adopt clear meeting practices experience noticeable shifts:

- Unnecessary meetings decrease
- Rework declines
- Decisions stick
- Feedback becomes easier
- Conflict becomes productive instead of personal
- Workflows become more predictable

And people feel something they haven't felt in a long time: space. The space to think. The space to lead. The space to be creative. The space to engage instead of react.

CLARITY BUILDS TRUST

Trust isn't built through big statements and vision documents. Trust is built in the small, repeated moments when people experience consistency and transparency. When purposes are named, people recognize that their time matters. When outcomes are visible, everyone knows what success looks like. When the right people are present, people know their expertise is valued.

This book is not just about designing meetings that produce results. It is about elevating leadership through clarity. When meetings become clear, everything around them becomes clear: priorities, expectations, decisions, relationships, and culture.

The CLEAR framework gives leaders a practical, repeatable way to design meetings that advance the work instead of stalling it. Each element builds on the next:

- **C**larify the purpose
- **L**ist the outcomes
- **E**ngage the right people
- **A**lign roles and expectations
- **R**elevance to them

Designing meetings that matter takes discipline and the skills you already have. When you design a meeting with clarity, you create the conditions for meaningful engagement and better ideas. And it begins with the next meeting you choose to design with intention.

CHAPTER 2 REFLECTION

Use these questions to deepen your thinking before you move on:

- When have unclear expectations caused rework, frustration, or delay?

- Where might I be assuming that my coworkers understand something that hasn't actually been shared?

- What signals do my communication habits send to my team?

- Which leadership habits could I strengthen to create more clarity in everyday work?

PART II

THE CLEAR FRAMEWORK

The **CLEAR** framework provides the structure leaders need to design meetings that create real progress. Part II introduces each element of the framework and shows how purpose, outcomes, people, roles, and relevance come together to transform how conversations unfold and how work moves forward.

THE *CLEAR* FRAMEWORK

Clarify the purpose

List the outcomes

Engage the right people

Align roles and expectations

Relevance to them

CHAPTER 3

CLARIFY THE MEETING PURPOSE

*If your purpose can't fit on a sticky note,
it's not clear enough.*

The global operations team had gathered for their weekly hybrid sync, a meeting meant to keep work aligned across regions. By the time everyone joined, the conversation had already split between the in-room side chatter and the small talk happening in the chat. The director in Houston opened with, "We have a lot to cover today," and immediately launched into a list of updates, none of which were connected. A manager from Curitiba asked if decisions were expected. Someone from Bangkok thought this meeting was for status reporting and had all her materials ready. Another believed they were reviewing priorities for the next sprint. One meeting. Three interpretations. No clear purpose.

Halfway through, the vice president joined the call, listened for a few minutes, and finally asked, "Why are we meeting right now? What do we need to walk away with?" The room fell silent. Not because people disagreed, but because no one had an answer. The meeting continued out of habit, and when it ended, no one could point to progress. Two people stayed behind to ask clarifying questions. One person started revising work based on assumptions that did not match the VP's expectations. It was a familiar pattern.

The next morning, the VP sent a short message to the leadership team. "Going forward, no meeting happens unless the purpose is stated upfront. If we do not know why we are meeting, we do not meet." That decision changed everything. Within weeks, the team began cancelling meetings that had no clear purpose, redesigned others, and approached conversations with greater intention. Productivity increased. So did morale. The shift began with a simple question: Why are we meeting?

Research shows that the deepest meeting frustration isn't what happens during the conversation. It's when people's expectations about the meeting aren't met. When the purpose is vague or assumed, people walk in with different mental models of what success looks like. One person thinks they're deciding. Another thinks they're reporting. Someone else thinks they're brainstorming. That mismatch is what slows teams down. A clear purpose realigns expectations so the group enters the room already pointed in the same direction.

"If the why is missing, the meeting should be too."

WHY PURPOSE MATTERS

Purpose is the anchor of every meeting. It defines the reason people are gathering, the work they are meant to do, and the outcome that moves the organization forward. Without it, meetings drift into information dumping, circular conversations, or updates that could have been shared asynchronously. With it, meetings become focused, actionable, and respectful of everyone's time.

A clear purpose does more than create efficiency. It creates boundaries that help people feel safe contributing. People show up with confidence when they understand why they are there and how they can contribute. It sets boundaries, reduces ambiguity, and gives permission for people to speak up when conversations veer off track. Purpose signals leadership intention.

When leaders consistently articulate purpose, teams trust that meetings exist for a reason, not out of routine.

Purpose also prevents rework. When people align on why they are meeting before they start, they make decisions that hold. They produce work that matches expectations. They avoid the endless back-and-forth caused by vague direction or mismatched assumptions. A clear purpose removes the guesswork from the start.

WHAT PURPOSE IS (AND WHAT IT IS NOT)

PURPOSE (WHY) → OUTCOMES (WHAT) → AGENDA (HOW)

Purpose is the reason the meeting exists. It is the outcome that the conversation is meant to advance. It is concise, specific, and directional.

Purpose is *not* the following:

- An agenda
- A description of the topic
- A list of talking points
- A vague aspiration like "talk about" or "touch base"

A clear purpose statement answers one question: Why do we need this meeting to move the work forward?

When the purpose is defined well, people know how to prepare and contribute, and whether they need to attend at all. Purpose clarifies the intent behind the meeting so the meeting design can serve it.

WHERE LEADERS STRUGGLE

Most leaders do not skip purpose intentionally; rather, they move so quickly that they assume people already know why they are meeting. They believe the recurring calendar invite speaks for itself. They rely on habit. Or they avoid stating a purpose because they are not fully sure themselves.

Sometimes leaders fear that defining purposes will make the meeting feel too rigid. They want to keep space open for collaboration, so they avoid naming a clear objective. Ironically, however, clarity increases collaboration because it creates shared boundaries and direction.

Other leaders face organizational pressure. Legacy meetings linger. Stakeholders expect updates, whether they are needed or not. People over-invite out of fear of leaving someone out. Each of these patterns dilutes clarity. The psychological truth is simple: when leaders are unclear, teams compensate with assumptions, and assumptions rarely take the team where it needs to go.

LEADER LANGUAGE

"Before we begin, let's restate why we're here today."

HOW TO GET PURPOSE RIGHT

Start with one sentence. You should be able to write it on a sticky note without running out of space.

A strong purpose statement includes the following:

1. A clear action: decide, prioritize, evaluate, plan, align

2. The focus of that action: the work or topic being shaped

3. Why it matters now: the context that makes the meeting necessary

Here are a few examples:

- Decide the final direction for the Q3 initiatives so teams can begin planning.

- Identify the root cause of delays in the onboarding workflow so improvement work can start.

- Align the team on next month's priorities so work can be staged with confidence.

- Align on the strategic update so leaders can deliver a unified message to the board.

Different meeting types require different levels of precision:

- Decision meetings need a purpose tied to a specific choice.

- Problem-solving meetings need a purpose tied to the core question being answered.

- Update meetings may not need to be meetings at all.

- Board meetings need a purpose tied to governance or strategic movement.

- Meetings in academic contexts like schools, colleges, and universities need a purpose tied to learning, policy, or progress.

AI can help you sharpen a fuzzy idea into a crisp, single-sentence purpose. It's especially useful for taking rough notes and shaping them into wording that reflects the qualities of a strong purpose. Try a prompt that includes the meeting context, your notes, and a reminder of what makes a purpose effective, followed by: "Draft a one-sentence meeting purpose that can fit on a single square sticky note." It's just a draft, though; review the output and revise as needed. You still decide the real purpose of the meeting: one that fits the moment, the people, and the stakes.

SHOULD THIS BE A MEETING?

Before gathering people, pause and ask yourself about the reason for bringing them together:

- If the purpose is to inform, send a message.

- If the purpose is to coordinate, use a shared document or task board.

- If the purpose is to align or decide, set up a meeting.

- If the purpose is unclear, wait. The meeting is not ready.

A meeting should only exist when the conversation advances work in a way that cannot happen asynchronously. Purpose determines necessity.

THE LINK TO CLEAR

Clarity about a meeting's purpose is the first element of CLEAR for a reason. It is the foundation on which every other part of meeting design rests. Without purpose, outcomes drift, engagement suffers, roles blur, and commitment weakens.

This is where intentional meetings begin. And it is where meaningful change begins.

CHAPTER 3 REFLECTION

Use these questions to deepen your thinking before you move on:

- What assumptions have I been making about why certain meetings exist?

- Which recurring meeting needs a rewritten purpose statement this week?

- How often am I using meetings for things that could be done another way?

- What would become possible if every meeting I led started with a one-sentence purpose statement?

CHAPTER 4

LIST THE DESIRED OUTCOMES

If you cannot name what success looks like,
you cannot create it.

The strategy team gathered for their quarterly planning session, a meeting everyone knew would be long. People from three time zones joined, some in a conference room in Singapore, others from Boston, Toronto, and London. The VP kicked things off with a hopeful tone. "We have a lot to accomplish today, but we will get through it. Let's walk through the deck."

What followed was a dense presentation with charts, insights, and a long list of work the department hoped to tackle. No one paused to define success. No one clarified what the group needed to walk away with by the end of their time together.

As the time passed, energy thinned. People began defending their priorities. Someone from London asked if the goal was alignment or decision-making. The Boston team thought they were selecting three strategic bets, while Toronto believed they were reviewing progress. Conversations became scattered. Every time someone suggested closing a topic, someone else asked, "But did we actually decide anything?"

Two hours in, the VP looked around and admitted, "I don't think we know what we're trying to achieve today." The group nodded silently. They were talking about the work without shaping outcomes that would move the work forward.

The meeting didn't suffer from a lack of effort. It suffered from a lack of outcomes—the clarity that defines what "done" looks like.

"If the outcome isn't clear, the meeting won't be either."

WHY OUTCOMES MATTER

If purpose is the "why" of the meeting, outcomes are the "what." They define what progress the group must create. They make expectations explicit. They prevent a meeting from becoming a place where ideas swirl without forming anything useful.

Studies show that unclear or incomplete outcomes increase decision latency—the delay between when a decision is needed and when it actually gets made. This delay compounds across teams, slowing projects, creating repeated conversations, and increasing frustration. When outcomes are explicit, decisions move faster because people know what they are working toward and what "done" looks like. Clear outcomes shorten the distance between discussion and action.

Knowing what success looks like reduces the mental load people carry. When people know what the meeting intends to produce, they understand how to contribute and when to speak up. They can challenge ideas respectfully because they are anchored to a shared destination. Outcomes turn a meeting from a loose conversation into a purposeful work session.

For leaders, outcomes serve as a tool of accountability and empowerment. When a leader articulates outcomes clearly, they give the group autonomy to focus and deliver. This creates speed. It prevents rework. It ensures that energy is directed toward what matters most. Strong outcomes create clarity that reaches far beyond the meeting itself.

WHAT OUTCOMES ARE (AND WHAT THEY ARE NOT)

TOPIC ≠ OUTCOME

Outcomes turn purpose into progress. They are the tangible results of the meeting. They describe what will exist at the end of the meeting that did not exist at the beginning.

Outcomes are the following:

- Decisions made
- Priorities set
- Plans created
- Agreements clarified
- Problems defined
- Risks evaluated
- Ideas refined

Outcomes must answer one question: What will be true at the end of this meeting? If the answer is unclear, the meeting is not ready.

COMMON PITFALLS LEADERS FACE

Leaders often skip outcomes because they believe defining them will limit conversation. In reality, the clearer the outcome, the freer the discussion. Without outcomes, meetings default to meandering dialogue and partially finished ideas.

Leaders also assume people know the outcomes without stating them directly. This is a common and costly mistake, as assumptions rarely align.

Another pitfall is trying to pack too many outcomes into one meeting. Leaders want to be efficient, so they try to accomplish everything at once. Instead of creating clarity, they create pressure. When the group feels rushed, quality suffers, and decisions lack confidence.

Some leaders avoid naming outcomes because they worry stakeholders will push back. They want to appear flexible. But flexibility without direction produces uncertainty. Clear outcomes don't restrict creativity; they protect it.

And then there is the emotional pitfall: leaders sometimes hesitate to define outcomes because they fear exposing misalignment. But misalignment doesn't disappear when avoided. It simply resurfaces later as rework, frustration, or slow execution.

LEADER LANGUAGE

"Before we move on, let's check whether we've met the outcomes we set."

HOW TO GET OUTCOMES RIGHT

Start with a simple formula: verb + object + context.
Here are some examples:

- Align on the top three Q3 priorities so teams can begin planning.

- Create a clear, validated problem statement so the group can begin root-cause analysis.

- Establish a shared view of next month's capacity so workload can be adjusted with confidence.

- Finalize the strategic update so leaders can deliver a unified message to the board members.

Outcomes should be stated before the meeting begins and repeated at the start of the meeting. They should be realistic for the time available. They should be specific enough that the group knows when they have been achieved.

Outcomes fall into different categories depending on the meeting's purpose:

Decision meetings
Outcomes should name the exact decision the group will make and what that decision will enable. This keeps the conversation focused and prevents drifting into unrelated analysis.

Problem-solving meetings
Outcomes should define the question the group is solving or the problem they are framing. This keeps the group centered on clarity rather than jumping to premature solutions.

Team meetings
Outcomes should clarify alignment—what the team will agree on, prioritize, or plan next. Team meetings move forward only when people have a shared understanding.

Board meetings
Outcomes should reflect governance and oversight. They should specify what the board will approve, review, endorse, or guide to ensure that the strategic direction is sound.

AI can help you turn draft outcomes into clearer, tighter language. It's especially useful when you want to ensure your wording connects to the purpose you've defined. Try a prompt that includes your meeting context and length, your draft list, and a reminder of what makes outcomes effective. Then prompt, "Refine these into a concise set of outcomes that describe what will be true by the end of the meeting." You still choose the outcomes that genuinely serve the group.

Once outcomes are set, they guide the meeting structure. Every agenda item must serve as an outcome. If it doesn't, it doesn't belong in the meeting.

SHOULD THIS BE A MEETING?

Outcomes also help you decide whether a meeting is even necessary. If the outcome is information-sharing only, don't schedule the meeting. If the outcome is a decision, meet only with the people essential to making that decision. If the outcome is unclear, clarify it before inviting anyone. If the outcome can be achieved in writing, choose writing. If the outcome requires real-time interaction, schedule the meeting.

A meeting should only exist when it is the best path to achieving the outcomes.

THE LINK TO CLEAR

Listing the desired outcomes is the second step of CLEAR because they bring the purpose to life. Purpose names the reason. Outcomes define the result. When leaders pair purpose with outcomes, meetings gain direction, momentum, and meaning. Teams stop guessing. They start producing.

This is how meetings become a force for progress rather than a drain on energy.

CHAPTER 4 REFLECTION

Use these questions to deepen your thinking before you move on:

- When have vague outcomes led to confusion or rework?

- What changes when my team knows exactly what we need to accomplish together?

- Which meeting this week needs rewritten outcomes?

- How can I practice stating outcomes before every meeting begins?

CHAPTER 5

ENGAGE THE RIGHT PEOPLE

If everyone is invited, no one is truly essential.

The product team met every Wednesday, a standard hybrid meeting designed to keep work aligned across engineering, product, program, and user experience domains. At first, the group included eight people. Over time, as new initiatives emerged and leaders wanted more visibility, the meeting ballooned. Twelve people joined. Then fifteen. Then nineteen. Half the camera squares remained off, and discussions became harder to manage. The meeting had shifted from a working session to a weekly progress review, with some people attending simply because they assumed they should be there.

During one session, the team attempted to finalize requirements for an upcoming feature, but every suggestion triggered a new tangent. Someone raised a concern from another department. Someone else questioned whether the meeting applied to their program at all. The program lead finally asked, "Do all of us need to be here for this decision?" The room went quiet. Not because people disagreed, but because no one had asked the question out loud before. The meeting ended without progress, and afterward, several attendees admitted privately that they had not needed to be there. They simply showed up because the invite appeared on their calendar.

This is how meeting bloat happens. It creeps in slowly. More people get added than removed. Attendance becomes a habit rather than a decision. Before long, the meeting serves everyone and no one at the same time. The team loses focus. Decisions slow down. Engagement drops.

"If the room is full of everyone, it won't be full of the right ones."

WHY ENGAGEMENT MATTERS

Research shows that meeting bloat rarely happens all at once. It grows through small, well-intended choices—inviting an extra stakeholder for visibility, adding someone "just in case," or keeping people on the list because they were included once before. Over time, these incremental additions create meetings that are larger than the work requires. When too many voices are present, conversations drift, ownership dilutes, and decisions become harder to make. Small, intentional choices about who is essential reverse this pattern.

Meetings do not need more people. They need the right people. Engaging the right people ensures that the conversation is informed, balanced, and effective. It prevents the noise that comes from inviting stakeholders who are curious but not responsible. It empowers the people who truly need to influence the decision. It respects the time of those who can contribute elsewhere.

When leaders invite the right people, contributors feel essential rather than peripheral, which increases participation. They challenge ideas with confidence. They bring diverse perspectives without overwhelming the meeting. The group becomes sharper because every voice in the room matters.

Engaging the right people is not about exclusivity. It is about effectiveness. Leaders often think that inviting more people increases transparency or reduces the risk of miscommunication. In reality, large working meetings dilute ownership. They create passivity. They shift accountability away from the people who need to make the decision and into the collective blur of a large group.

Engagement is not measured by who attends. It is measured by the number of people who can contribute meaningfully.

WHAT ENGAGEMENT IS (AND WHAT IT IS NOT)

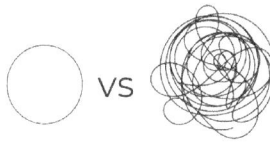

Engagement in meetings means having the right people present for the work the meeting is designed to accomplish. Those people understand why they are there and how they are expected to contribute. It also includes ensuring that the voices in the room reflect the perspectives necessary to provide relevant insights or make a strong decision without overwhelming the conversation.

Engagement is the following:

- The right minds in the room
- People contributing from their roles of responsibility
- Voices aligned to the decision, the problem, or the work
- A group small enough to think clearly and act decisively

Engagement is not the following:

- Broad invitations "just in case"
- Meetings overloaded with observers
- People joining out of obligation
- Filling seats for the sake of reputation

The question is not "Who wants to attend?" The right question to ask is, "Who is essential for this work?"

COMMON PITFALLS LEADERS FACE

Leaders struggle with this step for reasons that are more emotional than logistical. Many worry that not inviting someone will create political tension, damage a relationship, or signal disrespect. But inviting people to unnecessary meetings doesn't protect relationships. In fact, it often strains them. It wastes time, dilutes focus, and sends the message that having the "important" people in the room matters more than having the people essential to the work.

Others invite too many people because they want to avoid transparency issues. They believe that if everyone is in the room, no one can claim they were uninformed. This instinct is understandable, especially in complex environments. But transparency is not achieved through attendance. It is created through clear, timely communication.

Another pitfall is assuming that more voices automatically lead to better decisions. Large meetings rarely create more meaningful input; they create more noise. When too many people weigh in on a working meeting, the group spends more time reconciling opinions than solving the actual problem. The exception is a well-designed all-hands meeting, which is intentionally built for broad communication and engagement.

Finally, leaders fall into the trap of legacy invites. A person once needed to be involved, so they remain on the list long after their relevance has passed. Legacy invites slowly erode productivity.

LEADER LANGUAGE

"Who is essential for this discussion, and who can receive the summary instead?"

HOW TO GET ENGAGEMENT RIGHT

Start with the purpose and outcomes, as they determine who is necessary. Ask three questions:

- Who owns the decision? Decision-makers are essential. Everyone else is not.

- Who holds information that the group must use? If their knowledge or experience is critical to the conversation, they should be invited.

- Who will take action based on what is decided? If their work is directly shaped by the outcome, they need a seat at the table.

If someone is not essential to one of these categories, give them a summary instead of a seat.

Different meeting types require different engagement strategies:

Decision meetings
Keep the group small. Decision-makers and key advisors only.

Problem-solving meetings
Invite the subject-matter experts and those responsible for implementing the solution. Not everyone who touches the work needs to be in the room.

Standing team meetings
Include team members only. Interested stakeholders can be updated asynchronously.

Academic meetings
Engage people connected to curriculum, policy, outreach, or student impact, depending on the outcomes.

AI can help you brainstorm who might belong in the room by scanning your meeting purpose, outcomes, and the principles you've already considered for selecting participants. Try a prompt that includes your meeting context, the purpose and outcomes, and a short summary of your criteria for engagement. Then prompt, "Suggest who should attend and why based on these details." You still decide who actually needs to be in the room, because only you understand the people, the history, and the dynamics.

SHOULD THIS BE A MEETING?

Considering who should be engaged can help you determine whether a meeting should happen at all. If you cannot identify who is essential, the meeting is not ready. If the list of potential attendees keeps expanding, the meeting is too vague. If the meeting requires more observers than contributors, it can be a communication update. If the right people are unavailable and the work cannot move forward without them, reschedule or adapt the format.

A meeting should only occur when the right people can do the right work at the right time. Engagement is about intention, not invitation volume.

THE LINK TO CLEAR

"Engage the right people" is the third step of CLEAR because it determines the quality of every discussion that follows. Clarifying the purpose shows why the meeting exists. Listing the outcomes defines what it must create. Engaging the right people means you identify who must bring it to life.

When these three elements work together, meetings become focused and more meaningful. Teams gain confidence. Leaders gain credibility. Decisions gain momentum. This is how meeting culture begins to shift—from crowded and unclear to intentional and purposeful.

CHAPTER 5 REFLECTION

Use these questions to deepen your thinking before you move on:

- When have too many people slowed down a decision or diluted accountability?

- Who on my recurring meeting list is essential, and who may be attending out of habit?

- What would shift if I invited only the people required for the work at hand?

- How can I protect people's time by offering summaries instead of seats?

CHAPTER 6

ALIGN ROLES AND EXPECTATIONS

Tell people what is expected of
them before they walk in, not after

The small but fast-growing operations team met every Monday morning to kick off the week. The business had recently shifted to a hybrid model, with some team members coming into the office and others working remotely. The meeting was meant to create alignment and momentum, but instead, it often started with confusion. People joined without knowing whether they were expected to present, weigh in, or simply listen. The meeting began with polite greetings, followed by the team lead asking, "So… where should we start?" Every week felt slightly different. Every week, people guessed.

On one Monday, the uncertainty reached a breaking point. The team was reviewing a request from leadership to streamline a key process in the value stream. Several people arrived assuming this was an information-sharing meeting. Others came prepared to make decisions. One person thought they were responsible for bringing the process data. The team lead kept trying to move the discussion forward, but every question revealed another mismatch in expectations. Finally, a new analyst spoke up: "Can we pause? I am not sure who is responsible for what right now." The room fell quiet.

No one was confused because they lacked competence. They were confused because they lacked clarity.

When expectations are vague, participation becomes uneven. Some people dominate. Others withdraw. Decisions wobble.

Accountability blurs. The meeting ends, but the ambiguity continues long after people leave the room. Roles and expectations turn meetings from passive gatherings into active work sessions.

"If no one knows their role, confusion will gladly take the lead."

WHY ALIGNMENT MATTERS

Aligning roles and expectations is not about assigning tasks. It is about creating shared understanding. People contribute best when they know what is expected of them, how they can support the work, and what authority they hold in the conversation.

Clear expectations reduce cognitive load. People can focus on the work instead of decoding their place in the meeting. They step in with confidence, step back when appropriate, and collaborate with ease. When expectations are named upfront, surprises decrease and trust increases. This is one way clarity strengthens psychological safety: people know what to expect and what is expected of them.

Studies show that psychological safety forms through the small, predictable structures people experience every day. Clear expectations reduce uncertainty, which lowers anxiety and makes participation feel safer. When people understand their role and authority in the room, they speak up more confidently, challenge ideas more openly, and collaborate with greater ease. Structure does not limit contribution; it liberates it.

For leaders, alignment strengthens their ability to guide the group in a productive direction. Meetings run more smoothly, conversations stay focused, and conflict becomes easier to navigate. Alignment replaces guesswork with intention.

WHAT ROLES AND EXPECTATIONS ARE (AND WHAT THEY ARE NOT)

WHO IS HERE   ————————→   HOW THEY CONTRIBUTE
(ENGAGE)   (ALIGN)

Roles and expectations define the function each person plays and the level of contribution required from them in this specific meeting.

They answer the following questions:

- What is my role in this meeting?

- What am I responsible for contributing?

- What authority do I have in this decision?

Roles and expectations are *not* the following:

- Job titles

- Identity labels

- Broad responsibilities

- Vague statements like "be prepared to share"

A well-aligned meeting defines specific roles such as decision-maker, subject-matter expert, and challenger. They describe what the person is responsible for doing in the meeting. Not in general. Not someday. Now.

Most Common Roles:

- Facilitator (guides the process)

- Decision Owner (makes the call)

- Contributor (offers expertise and context)

- Challenger (tests ideas and assumptions)

COMMON PITFALLS LEADERS FACE

Leaders often hesitate to align roles and expectations because they assume people already know what is expected, especially in recurring meetings. But familiarity is not clarity. Even teams that work closely can misread expectations if they are not named.

Leaders also hesitate to set expectations when meetings involve multiple stakeholders or cross-functional partners. They worry about stepping on toes or implying hierarchy. But unclear authority creates more tension than naming it. When boundaries aren't stated, people become territorial, passive, or defensive.

And then there is the political layer. Leaders often feel pressure to invite "important" people, even when those individuals aren't essential to the work. No one wants to appear exclusionary. But adding people to avoid political fallout wastes time, dilutes focus, and sends the message that perceived importance matters more than involving the people who are actually needed to move the work forward. Aligning roles and expectations makes the third step in CLEAR easier; the meeting organizer knows who the right people to engage are.

LEADER LANGUAGE

"Here's how I'd like each of you to contribute today."

HOW TO ALIGN ROLES
AND EXPECTATIONS EFFECTIVELY

Before the meeting, answer these two questions:

1. What roles must exist for this meeting to succeed?
2. What must each role contribute?

Then communicate expectations clearly in the invitation, in the agenda, or at the start of the meeting. Roles and expectations should directly support the purpose and outcomes. They work together to create momentum.

Here are a few examples:

- "Lin will make the final decision after hearing input."
- "Sofia and Jim will walk us through the data and answer questions."
- "Ben and Charlie will challenge assumptions and raise risks."
- "I will facilitate, track time, and keep us focused on the outcomes."
- "Everyone else is a contributor."

Different meeting types require different expectations:

Decision meetings
Clarify who decides, who advises, and who informs. The decision-makers must be obvious.

Problem-solving meetings
Define who brings data, who frames the issue, and who tests assumptions.

Cross-functional meetings
Clarify who has decision authority. Without this, discussions drift, and people advocate for their function instead of the shared outcome.

Academic meetings
Define what faculty, staff, and administrators need to bring to the conversation.

Partner with your AI to draft simple role descriptions or expectations that reflect the guidance you've already created for the meeting. Try a prompt that includes your meeting purpose, outcomes, list of attendees, and their titles, and then ask: "What expectations for each person will help shape a collaborative discussion?" You still define what is needed to make the conversation successful.

SHOULD THIS BE A MEETING?

Roles and expectations reveal whether a meeting is necessary. If no one knows who is responsible, the meeting is not ready. If too many people hold the same role, change up the expectations or reconsider whom to engage so there is balance. If authority is unclear, clarify it before scheduling the meeting. If expectations can't be named, the meeting is not ready.

A meeting should only occur when the roles and expectations support the purpose and outcomes.

THE LINK TO CLEAR

"Align roles and expectations" is the fourth step of CLEAR because it turns clarity into action. Clarifying the purpose states the reason. Listing the outcomes defines success. Engagement brings the right people. Aligning roles and expectations tells those people how to contribute.

When leaders create alignment on roles and expectations, meetings become grounded in purpose and value. People step into their responsibilities, decisions sharpen, and accountability becomes natural. Trust grows inside the meeting, and progress becomes repeatable.

CHAPTER 6 REFLECTION

Use these questions to deepen your thinking before you move on:

- Which of my meetings lack clarity about who decides, who informs, who challenges, and who contributes?

- How often do I assume people know their role without naming it?

- What would happen if I made roles and expectations explicit at the start of each meeting?

- How can this clarity strengthen psychological safety on my team?

.

CHAPTER 7

RELEVANCE TO THEM

If you cannot articulate the benefit,
you cannot expect commitment.

The board gathered around a long conference table, the early morning light spilling across a row of neatly printed briefing binders. This meeting had been on the calendar for weeks. People traveled, cleared schedules, and rearranged commitments to be present. The CEO opened with gratitude and then launched into a review of the strategic initiative she hoped the board would support.

For the first twenty minutes, the room was attentive but passive. The information was thorough, but the energy was flat. The update explained the driving factors that led to the initiative. It did not explain why this conversation mattered now or how the board's participation would influence what happened next. A few people scribbled notes. Others listened politely. No one leaned forward. No one asked questions. No one engaged.

Finally, the board chair asked, "If we give this our full attention today, what will we, as a board, be better equipped to do? And why does this discussion deserve our focus right now?" It was a reasonable question, and it revealed the gap.

The CEO knew she needed direction and alignment. What she had not clarified was why that alignment mattered to them as a board—how this conversation would strengthen their ability to govern effectively, reduce risk, or guide the organization's future with confidence. She had not framed the benefit, the relevance, the meaning. Without that, attendance became presence without purpose. People commit and engage in meetings when they see value in them.

"If the meeting doesn't matter to them, their attention won't either."

Many employees do not understand the benefit of the meetings that flood their calendars. They show up, but they do not lean in. They listen, but they are not fully invested. They participate, but only on the surface. Not because they are disengaged, but because the relevance to them was never communicated.

Relevance to them is the motivation behind the meeting—the part that makes the meeting matter to the people in the room.

WHY RELEVANCE TO THEM MATTERS

Relevance to them is how people make sense of where to put their time, attention, and energy. This is not about selfishness. Time is a finite commodity, and how we spend our time matters.

When leaders clearly articulate why a meeting matters to the people they invite, the following things occur:

- Engagement rises
- Ownership strengthens
- Ideas surface
- Collaboration feels natural

When relevance to them is missing, even the most well-designed meeting struggles. People attend physically but disengage mentally. They withhold ideas and contribute narrowly. The work may move forward, but it does so without full commitment and buy-in.

Relevance to them creates the emotional connection needed for meaningful participation. It turns obligation into choice and attendance into investment.

WHAT RELEVANCE TO THEM IS
(AND WHAT IT IS NOT)

YOU WILL...
▼
THIS HELPS YOU...
▼
YOUR PERSPECTIVE MATTERS BECAUSE...

Relevance to them is the personal meaning of the meeting—the answer to the silent question every human being brings into the meeting: Why should I dedicate my time, thinking, influence, and energy to this conversation?

Relevance to them is the following:

- The clear benefit for the person attending

- The value they gain

- The insight they walk away with

- The influence they get to shape

- The problem that becomes easier because they showed up

Relevance to them is *not* the following:

- A generic "the boss said this is important"

- A broad appeal to organizational goals with no personal connection

- A hope that people will connect the dots themselves

Relevance to them must be specific and personal. If it is not, it disappears.

COMMON PITFALLS LEADERS FACE

Even well-designed meetings fall flat when relevance is unspoken.

Just because someone works at an organization does not mean that every meeting they are invited to must be of value to them. People need to understand why the meeting matters to their work, influence, or success.

One common pitfall is that leaders focus heavily on the agenda or the content, but do not pause to consider the attendees' perspectives. They outline topics and talking points, but they do not translate those elements into personal relevance. When leaders assume the meeting's importance is self-evident, people show up out of obligation rather than interest. Without a clear reason to attend, engagement becomes passive even when the topic itself is strategic.

Another challenge surfaces when leaders communicate what they need from attendees but overlook what the attendees will gain. This creates a dynamic where people feel they are being asked to contribute without receiving anything meaningful in return. Meetings become extractive rather than beneficial. Over time, this pattern erodes enthusiasm and weakens psychological safety

LEADER LANGUAGE

*"Here's why your voice matters
in this conversation."*

because people sense their participation is being used, not valued.

The key thing to remember is simple: people support what supports them. They invest in what brings value to them. Make it clear.

HOW TO GET RELEVANCE TO THEM RIGHT

Getting relevance to them right requires intention before the meeting ever begins. Leaders must consider not only what the meeting needs to produce, but also what each person will walk away with that makes their job easier, their decisions clearer, or their influence more meaningful.

Relevance to them is the emotional permission people need to invest fully. When leaders name the benefit directly, people feel respected before the meeting even begins.

You can start with a simple structure:

- What they will gain from participating: "You will help shape the final direction before we go to market."

- Why their perspective matters: "Your experience with customer feedback will help us avoid major risks."

- What will become easier for them because of this meeting: "This decision will remove ambiguity for your team for the next quarter."

Different types of meetings require different expressions of "relevance to them":

Decision meetings
"You shape the final choice. Your voice determines our direction."

Problem-solving meetings
"You will gain clarity on what is causing friction and what to do about it."

Team meetings
"You will leave knowing what to focus on and how to succeed this month."

Academic meetings
"You help ensure our decisions support students and our long-term learning goals."

People need to understand how attending this meeting makes something better for them, their team, or their work.

Partner with AI to translate your notes into clear, tailored statements that reflect what issues are relevant in the meeting. After providing it with the context of the first four terms of CLEAR and your notes, try a prompt like "Draft 1–2 sentences explaining why this meeting matters to each attendee. Be specific about how they will benefit from participating." You still bring the insight and empathy needed to know what truly resonates with each person.

SHOULD THIS BE A MEETING?

Relevance to them is one of the most reliable indicators of whether a meeting should exist at all. If a leader cannot articulate why someone benefits from attending, the meeting is not ready. If the relevance feels generic or forced, the conversation may be better handled asynchronously. When people gain nothing from being present, the meeting becomes a drain on time and energy.

When relevance to them is strong and specific, people arrive with clarity, motivation, and a sense of purpose. They know exactly why they are there, and they are far more likely to contribute meaningfully.

A meeting without relevance to them is a meeting people endure, not a meeting they engage in.

THE LINK TO CLEAR

Relevance to them completes CLEAR by bringing humanity into the meeting. Clarifying the purpose tells people why the meeting exists. Listing the outcomes defines what will be created. Engaging the right people identifies who must be present. Aligning roles and expectations tells people how to contribute.

Relevance to them tells them why it matters to them. It turns clarity into commitment and structure into motivation.

When relevance to them is expressed clearly, people step into the meeting with intention rather than obligation. They bring insight, energy, and ownership. Conversations deepen. Decisions strengthen. Trust grows. People feel valued, not just invited. Relevance to them turns a meeting into a moment that matters.

CHAPTER 7 REFLECTION

Use these questions to deepen your thinking before you move on:

- Do the people I invite understand what they will gain from attending my meetings?

- How often do I assume the relevance is obvious rather than saying it out loud?

- What could I communicate before my next meeting to increase commitment and engagement?

- How would my meetings change if everyone knew how their presence benefited them?

CHAPTER 8

THE CLEAR AGENDA
Let your agenda do the work.

Most agendas are built out of habit. They list the topics people want to cover, the updates someone needs to share, and the items that have carried over from previous meetings. These agendas look tidy, but they rarely help teams move work forward. They create the illusion of structure, not the experience of progress.

A CLEAR agenda is different. It begins with intention, not topics. It guides conversation rather than cataloging content. It reflects what the group must accomplish rather than what each person wants to discuss.

CLEAR gives leaders the inputs. The agenda turns those inputs into a practical structure that helps the group succeed. A strong agenda turns clarity into direction.

START WITH THE PURPOSE AND OUTCOMES

Every agenda should begin with the following two elements:

1. Why the meeting exists

2. What must be created by the end of it

This framing sets the tone. It helps people arrive prepared. It signals that the meeting is grounded in results, not routine.

If these two elements are missing, the meeting is at risk before it even starts. If they are present and visible, the group already has a shared anchor.

Keep them at the top of the agenda, not buried in an email or implied. When purpose and outcomes are visible, alignment increases naturally.

LET OUTCOMES DRIVE THE STRUCTURE

A CLEAR agenda lists outcomes in the order they must be achieved. This small shift changes everything. If the leader thinks only in terms of the topic under discussion, the meeting structure can end up being vague and unfocused.

Topic-based agenda:

1. Product update

2. Launch discussion

3. Risks

4. Timeline

Outcome-based agenda:

1. Confirm what is ready for launch

2. Decide on the launch date

3. Identify risks that need mitigation

4. Agree on the communication plan

The outcome-based version tells people what success looks like. It helps them think more strategically. It makes time use visible. It creates clearer boundaries for discussion.

Outcomes are the skeleton of the agenda. Everything else supports the structure.

CLARIFY ROLES AND TIMEBOXES

Once outcomes shape the flow, add the elements that make the meeting efficient and psychologically safe:

- Who will guide each section

- Who holds the decision authority

- Where discussion, ideation, or decision is expected

- How much time is allocated for each segment

Timeboxes don't make meetings rigid; they protect the work. They communicate boundaries and keep people from wandering into unrelated territory. Timeboxes also help groups build trust and learn to communicate succinctly. When people know what to expect, they participate more confidently.

INCLUDE RELEVANCE TO THEM IN THE INVITE, NOT THE AGENDA

Relevance to them doesn't need to sit on the agenda itself, but it does need to be clearly stated in the meeting invitation. One sentence is enough to help them prepare and participate purposefully:

- "You will leave with final alignment on next quarter's priorities, so your team can plan with confidence."

- "You'll have the chance to shape the direction before decisions are locked in."

TWO EXAMPLES OF CLEAR AGENDAS

Agenda Example #1
Strategic Leadership Team
Quarterly Alignment Meeting

Purpose: Align on next quarter's priorities so the org can move into planning with clarity and confidence

Outcomes:
1. Confirm organizational priorities for the upcoming quarter
2. Assign decision owners for each priority to ensure accountability
3. Identify risks and resource needs that could impact execution
4. Agree on next steps for communicating decisions to the broader organization

Agenda:

1. Set the Frame (5 min)
   - Review purpose, outcomes, roles
2. Outcome 1: Confirm organizational priorities (20 min)
   - Lead: COO | Format: Discussion → Decision
3. Outcome 2: Assign decision ownership (5 min)
   - Lead: CEO | Contributors: All ELT
4. Outcome 3: Identify risks + resource needs (15 min)
   - Lead: HR + Finance | Format: Round-the-room
5. Outcome 4: Agree on communication plan + next steps (10 min)
   - Lead: Communications
- Visible Summary + Owners (5 min)

Agenda Example #2
Higher Education 4DX Team Check-In

Purpose: Review progress toward our WIGs so the team can make focused commitments for the week ahead

Outcomes:
1. Report progress against lead measures with visibility across all faculty teams.
2. Identify breakthrough commitments that will move the WIGs forward this week.
3. Surface barriers that require support or escalation.
4. Confirm shared actions and owners

Agenda:

1. Set the Frame (5 min)
   - Review purpose, outcomes, scoreboard
2. Outcome 1: Report on lead measures (10 min)
   - Lead: Team Lead | Format: Rapid updates
3. Outcome 2: Identify breakthrough commitments (15 min)
   - Lead: Team Members | Format: Group brainstorm - Selection
4. Outcome 3: Surface barriers (10 min)
   - Lead: Dean/Assoc. Dean | Format: Open
5. Outcome 4: Confirm shared actions + owners (5 min)

If you would like help applying CLEAR to your team's meetings or designing agendas for your organization's unique rhythms, I would be happy to partner with you. No meeting is one-size-fits-all, and the most powerful agendas are shaped with teams in mind.

THE CLEAR AGENDA CHECKLIST

Before finalizing an agenda, ask the following questions:

- Does the agenda begin with purpose and outcomes?
- Are all items outcome-based rather than topic-based?
- Is the order logical and necessary?
- Are roles and decisions clear?
- Is the time realistic and respectful?
- Does everyone understand the relevance to them before they arrive?
- Will this agenda lead to meaningful progress?

If the answer to all is yes, the agenda is CLEAR.

CHAPTER 9

BRINGING CLEAR
TO LIFE IN THE ROOM

Design sets the plan. Facilitation brings it to life.

CLEAR gives you the structure to create intentional, outcome-driven meetings. But once people enter the room, physically or virtually, your role shifts from designer to facilitator. And that role requires a different kind of awareness. Facilitating a meeting is about holding the frame with clarity while making space for people to think, speak, challenge, and decide together.

This chapter offers a handful of essential facilitation practices that elevate CLEAR from a design framework to a lived experience. These are not advanced techniques. They are foundational habits leaders can use in real time to help the room do its best thinking.

Use these notes to sharpen your presence, deepen your impact, and strengthen the culture you're shaping with CLEAR.

PREPARE THE ROOM BEFORE PEOPLE ENTER

I hope by now you realize that facilitation begins before the meeting starts. A strong meeting experience comes from giving people what they need to participate meaningfully. This can include sharing the purpose and outcomes in advance, clarifying any pre-work, identifying decisions that will be made, and naming the roles people will play. It also involves ensuring that the space is ready: the tools that people will need are present, the tech is functioning as expected, and everyone has a place to sit. When people arrive prepared, conversations have a great chance of success. Preparation sets the stage, design shapes the experience, and facilitation brings it to life. Together, they're the foundation of every successful meeting.

HOLD THE STRUCTURE GENTLY BUT FIRMLY

CLEAR gives you the architecture; facilitation keeps people inside it without shutting them down. Holding the structure is an act of stewardship, not control.

When you restate the purpose at the beginning, keep outcomes visible, or pause the room to ask whether a tangent belongs today, you help people stay aligned with the work they came to do. A good facilitator protects the frame so people can contribute freely without losing direction.

Experiment with a grounding phrase like: "Let's pause and reconnect to our outcomes. Are we still moving toward them?"

INVITE BALANCED PARTICIPATION

Meetings thrive when the right voices contribute in the right ways. Not when everyone speaks for an equal amount of time, but when everyone has the opportunity to be heard and shape the work.

Some people need encouragement to speak; others need boundaries. A facilitator notices who the group defaults to, who hasn't spoken, and who may be unintentionally over-influencing the room.

Here are two simple moves to experiment with:

- Ask quieter people early: "What's one thing on your mind as we begin?"
- Redirect dominant voices graciously: "Let's pause and hear from someone we haven't heard yet."

MAKE HYBRID HUMANS VISIBLE

Hybrid is now the norm, but most meetings still privilege those in the room. Facilitation requires intentionally leveling the playing field.

Research shows that hybrid meetings often create participation gaps. People joining remotely tend to contribute less, feel less heard, and experience greater cognitive strain than those physically in the room. Without intentional facilitation, remote participants become observers rather than contributors. The meeting structure must make participation possible for everyone, not just those sitting closest to the facilitator.

Invite remote voices first at key moments. Pause longer so virtual participants can unmute.

Experiment with these verbal check-ins:

- "Remote folks, how's this landing for you?" or
- "Let's kick off our ideation by hearing from the remote folks first."

SLOW DOWN WHEN IT MATTERS

Fast meetings are not the same as effective meetings. When stakes rise or tensions surface, many leaders instinctively speed up, hoping to move past the discomfort quickly. Strong facilitators do the opposite. They slow the room down just enough to help people think rather than react.

Tension is not a bad thing. It is information. It often signals competing priorities, unspoken assumptions, or emerging insights. Trying to shut it down too quickly can silence important perspectives and weaken decisions.

Experiment with simple ways to hold space for healthy debate:

- "I'm noticing some tension here. Let's name what feels different in our perspectives so we can understand it."

- "What would you like to see happen?"
- "What's one action we can agree to as a next step?"

SUMMARIZE TO CLOSE LOOPS

People assume shared understanding far more often than they actually have it. Facilitation closes loops explicitly so the group knows what is carried forward.

Experiment with these useful phrases:

- "Here's what I'm hearing us decide…"
- "Let's recap the two insights we're carrying forward…"
- "Before we move on, does this summary reflect where we landed?"

ANCHOR DIALOGUE IN OUTCOMES

When the conversation drifts (and it will), the facilitator returns the group to the outcomes without judgment. You are not correcting people. You are realigning the work.

People trust facilitators who can redirect without shutting down participation. Over time, the team starts doing this themselves because focus and clarity become a shared responsibility.

Experiment with these phrases:

- "How does this fit into our current purpose and outcomes?"
- "How does this idea connect back to the main outcomes we're here to work on?"
- "Would you be ok parking that topic so we can stay focused on our outcomes?

USE QUESTIONS THAT CREATE THINKERS

Questions are a facilitator's sharpest tool. A strong question opens thinking, helps a group get unstuck, clarifies intention, surfaces insight, and guides the discussion toward meaningful progress.

Experiment with questions that pair naturally with CLEAR:

- "What problem are we really solving right now?"
- "What decision are we trying to make in this moment?"
- "What do we still need to solve for today?"
- "What are the next steps to address this?"

PROTECT PSYCHOLOGICAL SAFETY IN REAL TIME

Clarity fuels psychological safety, and facilitation maintains it. When someone is interrupted, misunderstood, or dismissed, the facilitator repairs the moment.

Experiment with phrases like the following:

- "Let's make space for them to finish."
- "I want to make sure we heard that correctly—can you restate your key point?"
- "Two perspectives are emerging here. Let's understand both before we move forward."

END WITH INTENTION

Many meetings drift into vague agreement or end quickly without real closure. A facilitator brings closure that reinforces everything CLEAR stands for.

Experiment with these strong endings:

- A clear recap
- Confirmed owners of next steps
- A brief reflection: "Did we accomplish what we came for today?"

THE ESSENCE OF FACILITATION IN CLEAR

You don't need to be a master facilitator to run an effective meeting. You do need to hold the structure, invite balanced participation, manage the energy of the room, and help people create shared meaning. Experiment with these facilitation moves and observe the impact they have on your meetings.

CLEAR gives you the design. Facilitation gives you the impact. Together, they turn meetings into moments that matter.

PART III

SUSTAINING THE CHANGE

Clarity becomes powerful only when it becomes routine. Part III explores how teams embed CLEAR into daily practice, reinforcing new habits until they evolve into shared norms that strengthen focus, trust, and collaboration across the organization.

CHAPTER 10

PUTTING CLEAR INTO ACTION

Clarity grows through repetition.

Most leaders understand CLEAR the moment they hear it. The logic is intuitive. The steps make sense. The benefits are obvious. But understanding a framework is different from using it. And when the calendar fills, priorities shift, or pressure rises, leaders often slip back into familiar patterns: default agendas, habitual invites, unclear expectations, and conversations that drift.

The real work begins when CLEAR moves from theory to practice. The question leaders ask most often is "Where do I start?" The answer is simpler than it seems. You begin with one meeting. One moment of design. One choice to bring clarity into a room that has been operating without it.

When leaders do this, even once, the difference is immediate. Meetings feel lighter. Conversations focus more quickly. People contribute confidently. Clarity becomes something people can feel, not just understand. And once a team experiences that shift, they want more of it.

WHY PUTTING CLEAR INTO PRACTICE MATTERS

Understanding CLEAR intellectually is not the same as applying it. Most leaders already believe in the need for better meetings. They understand purpose matters. They know outcomes help. They have seen what happens when the wrong people are invited or when roles are unclear. The challenge is not awareness. The challenge is applying these behaviors under pressure.

Busy calendars, tight deadlines, and competing priorities create a pull toward familiar behaviors: inviting too many people, skipping outcomes, and hoping the discussion will naturally converge. In these moments, leaders often revert to what is easiest in the moment rather than what is clearest in the long run.

Putting CLEAR into practice interrupts that cycle. It creates a pause before people are invited. It slows the impulse to gather people without preparation. It asks leaders to think not only about what they want to accomplish, but about how the meeting needs to be structured for people to succeed.

This intentionality may feel awkward at first. New practices often do. But it becomes easier each time it is used. And most importantly, people feel the difference immediately.

STARTING SMALL

Using CLEAR does not require an overhaul of your entire meeting ecosystem at once. Change rarely succeeds through sweeping redesigns. What works is beginning where clarity will have the most impact: with one meeting you genuinely care about.

Start with the meeting that frustrates you the most. Or the one where decisions drift. Or the one where too many people attend without contributing. Or simply the next meeting on your calendar. Change begins with practice.

Clarify the purpose of the meeting you pick. What is the meeting for? Not what it covers, but what it must accomplish. Write it in a single sentence. Then identify the outcomes. What will be created, decided, or resolved by the end? Once these are clear, add them to the invitation. Say them aloud at the beginning of the meeting. This single act changes the frame. It communicates that the meeting exists for a reason and that people's time is being treated with intention.

Next, look at the attendee list. Who is essential to achieving the outcomes? Who is included because of habit or hierarchy?

Who can receive a summary instead of attending? Removing someone from a meeting is not an exclusion. It is an act of respect, when communicated thoughtfully.

Roles and expectations follow naturally. If everyone tends to agree too quickly, invite a "challenger" to spark debate and surface new perspectives. During ideation sessions, hold firm that all ideas are welcome until the group is ready to narrow. Clear expectations reduce the friction of participation. They eliminate the awkward moments when people look around, wondering who should speak next or who has the authority to decide. When expectations are stated, people contribute comfortably and confidently.

Relevance to them brings it all home. What benefit does each person receive by being at the meeting? How will the conversation help them move forward? People are willing to invest energy when they understand why the meeting matters to them. When people understand how the meeting benefits them, you get a better version of them in the room.

Take one meeting and make it CLEAR. The power of starting small is that it allows teams to see the results quickly. A focused meeting that ends early. A decision made after months of circular conversation. A team that leaves knowing exactly what to do next. The simplicity of CLEAR is what makes it sustainable. You do not need to be perfect. You only need to be intentional.

WHAT TEAMS NOTICE FIRST

When leaders begin applying CLEAR, teams typically notice a few immediate shifts:

- Meetings start on time.
- People arrive more prepared.
- Conversations feel more focused.
- Fewer voices dominate.
- Decisions are made with less hesitation.

These early wins matter. They show people what clear meetings feel like. They help teams see that clarity is not about rigid structure but about direction, relevance, and respect.

Most importantly, they build confidence in their ability to drive the change they need in their meeting culture. Conversations feel less chaotic and more productive. Meetings stop being a source of frustration and start becoming tools where real progress happens.

PRINCIPLES FOR PRACTICING CLEAR

As you bring CLEAR into your organization, a few principles will support your success:

Be open to experimentation.
Change does not happen through intention alone. Action is required.

Practice out loud.
State the purpose, outcomes, roles, and relevance in the room. Do not assume people already know them.

Set boundaries.
If a topic arises that does not support the outcomes, park it. Not every topic belongs in every meeting.

Invite reflection.
At the end of a meeting, take a minute to ask, "Did we achieve our outcomes?" and "What should we adjust next time?" Reflection creates improvement.

Give grace.
Teams will slip back into old habits at times. So will you. This is normal. Clarity grows through returning, not perfection.

Celebrate clarity.

When a meeting ends early or a decision sticks, acknowledge it. These moments reinforce the behavior you want to sustain.

LOOKING AHEAD

As leaders and teams integrate CLEAR into daily practice, a shift starts to happen. Meetings move from tactical obligations to purposeful conversations. People feel more confident in how they show up and more connected to why they are there. Decisions become easier, and the work becomes clearer.

But putting CLEAR into practice is only the beginning. To sustain the momentum, leaders must understand how to turn early wins into consistent behaviors and shared norms. The next chapter explores how clarity becomes a daily practice that strengthens every meeting and builds momentum for you and your team.

CHAPTER 10 REFLECTION

Use these questions to deepen your thinking before you move on:

- Which meeting this week is the best place to practice CLEAR?

- How might stating the purpose and outcomes out loud shift the tone of that meeting?

- What small win would help my team feel the value of clarity?

- What habit of mine needs to shift first for CLEAR to take hold?

CHAPTER 11

CREATING MEETING HABITS THAT STICK

Change happens when clarity becomes routine.

The first time the program management team used CLEAR, the shift was noticeable. The meeting felt calmer. People stopped talking over one another. The work moved forward instead of sideways. But the most important moment didn't happen in that meeting—it happened the following week, when the team lead opened the agenda and said aloud, "Let's begin with our purpose and outcomes."

It was the repetition that mattered, not the excitement of trying something new. The repetition signaled that clarity was becoming a habit. Over the next few weeks, the room grew more focused. Discussions became easier to navigate. People anticipated the structure and arrived ready for it.

This is how meeting culture begins to shift. Not all at once. Not through a sweeping transformation. But through small, steady choices that reinforce clarity again and again.

WHY DAILY PRACTICE MATTERS

A single CLEAR meeting is helpful. A pattern of CLEAR meetings is transformative. But patterns don't form on their own. They emerge when clarity is practiced in small, repeatable ways, especially when the old habits try to resurface.

Every team lives with invisible meeting habits: rushing into agendas, sending legacy invites, skipping purpose, letting conversations drift. These habits persist not because they are effective, but because they are familiar. The moment people get busy or tired or stressed, they default to what they know.

Daily practice disrupts that default. It invites teams to pause before choosing the path of least resistance. It reinforces the belief that meetings can be better, easier, and more respectful of people's time. It helps leaders and teams build confidence in behaviors that support good meetings. Daily practice is what turns a framework into a way of working.

RETURNING TO PURPOSE AND OUTCOMES

One of the strongest daily habits a team can build is returning to purpose and outcomes again and again. It sounds simple, even obvious, but it is one of the hardest disciplines to maintain.

Clarifying the purpose answers the question, "Why are we gathered?"

Listing the outcomes answers, "What must we produce before we leave?"

When meetings drift, and they will, returning to these anchors resets the conversation without shutting it down. It helps people reorient without judgment. It brings the group back into alignment.

When a team practices this enough times, something important happens: team members start doing it themselves. They say things like, "I want to make sure this connects to our outcomes." "Before we go further, which decision are we making?" "Is this part of today's purpose or something we should park?" Clarity becomes a shared responsibility instead of something the meeting owner tries to manage alone. And meetings become easier when everyone helps hold the frame.

CREATING A CONSISTENT RHYTHM

Daily practice is as much about rhythm as it is about content. When meetings begin and end with clarity, people know what to expect. They show up more prepared because the meeting structure is predictable.

A consistent rhythm sounds like the following:

- Purpose and outcomes at the beginning

- Alignment and confirmation at the end

- A brief pause when conversation drifts

- A moment of reflection after decisions

This rhythm builds trust. It signals that time will not be wasted, that conversations will be guided, and that people can bring their full attention without bracing for chaos. Predictability reduces anxiety and increases confidence. Rhythm makes meetings feel stable even when the work is complex.

DEVELOPING SHARED NORMS

As teams practice CLEAR, shared norms begin to emerge naturally. These norms are not formal rules written in handbooks. They are unspoken agreements reinforced through repetition and shared experience.

Norms often appear in the following ways:

- We start with purpose.

- We keep outcomes visible.

- We only invite the people who need to be there.

- We return to the frame when we drift.

- We name why the meeting matters to the people in the room.

- We confirm next steps before adjourning.

These norms help people understand how the team collaborates. They reduce friction and eliminate guesswork. When someone new joins the team, they learn very quickly: clarity and focus are how we work here.

These norms are the heartbeat of sustained clarity. They quietly reveal the culture a team is building, how they think, how they communicate, and what they value in their daily interactions. As these norms strengthen, they begin to shape not only how meetings run, but which meetings happen at all.

THE FREEDOM TO DECLINE THOUGHTFULLY

One of the most powerful habits that emerges from a daily CLEAR practice is the confidence to decline meetings thoughtfully. Specifically, people decline meetings when their expertise is not central to the outcomes, or their presence will not influence the decision, or when the conversation can be handled asynchronously. When people discern that their time is better invested elsewhere, it is appropriate and healthy to decline the invite.

Declining with clarity strengthens the meeting culture. It allows the meeting to move forward with the right people in a focused conversation to achieve outcomes. It invites the meeting owner to reflect on their intentions for the meeting to determine if a revisit of the CLEAR guidance is needed. It gives the person time back to focus on work priorities.

The reason behind the decline gives the organizer important information. And when leaders accept declines with respect, psychological safety rises. Teams learn that clarity is more important than presence.

OVERCOMING THE PULL OF OLD PATTERNS

Every team will experience moments when clarity gets lost. The meeting starts late. The purpose is skipped. The outcomes are assumed. Someone derails the conversation. People multitask. The old rhythm reappears. This is the natural friction of change. The key is returning, without judgment or drama, to the new CLEAR meeting pattern.

A simple question like "What outcome are we working toward right now?" can bring the group back. It is important to reflect, ideally with the group, on what could be improved the next time to create the meeting environment desired.

LOOKING AHEAD

Daily practice strengthens teams. But for clarity to reshape how an organization works, it must be reinforced by the people with the greatest reach and influence. Leaders who model clarity become catalysts. They not only deepen it for their team; they also accelerate it across the entire system. The next chapter explores how leaders reinforce clarity and turn it into a cultural norm that shapes how people collaborate, communicate, and make decisions.

CHAPTER 11 REFLECTION

Use these questions to deepen your thinking before you move on:

- What meeting habit do I need to shift to strengthen clarity on my team?

- Which meeting would improve immediately if I revisited the purpose, outcomes, or relevance to them?

- How can I model the freedom to decline meetings respectfully and thoughtfully?

- How will I keep myself and my team motivated when old patterns surface?

CHAPTER 12

CLARITY AS CULTURE

Culture shifts when leaders model clarity.

The finance IT team expected another long planning session—a familiar cycle of updates, debates, and slow decisions. Instead, their leader walked to the whiteboard and wrote five words across the top: Purpose. Outcomes. People. Roles. Relevance. She didn't make a speech. She simply named what the meeting needed to succeed and invited the group to build it together.

What happened over the next few hours wasn't dramatic. But it was different. Conversations stayed grounded. Decisions felt less personal and more principled. People spoke with more confidence because they understood their role and the work ahead. By the end, one team member said quietly, "I didn't realize how much mental clutter we were carrying until today."

That's the power of leadership modeling. When leaders show what clarity looks like, consistently and visibly, teams adopt it. The behavior spreads. And what starts in meetings becomes the rhythm of the culture itself.

WHY LEADERSHIP IS THE CATALYST

Meeting clarity becomes a cultural norm when leaders demonstrate it consistently through everyday behaviors. When leaders use CLEAR, teams internalize it. They have the language to lean on in their conversations. When leaders skip using CLEAR, teams learn that clarity is optional.

Whether leaders realize it or not, people are always watching. They pay attention to how decisions get made, how priorities are set, and how meetings are run. They notice whether psychological safety is genuine, how conflict is handled, and which behaviors are rewarded or quietly ignored. These cues become the unwritten rules that guide how the organization works.

The behaviors leaders model are what get magnified throughout the organization. This is why cultural change doesn't begin with policies or training. It begins with leaders showing people how clarity works in practice, first in meetings, then in conversations, and eventually in the organization's shared language.

HOW LEADERS MODEL CLARITY

Leaders do not need to be perfect to have an impact. They just need to be intentional. The leaders who create lasting cultural clarity often demonstrate a few consistent behaviors. They frame discussions before they begin. They make decisions visible. They use questions to anchor clarity. When conversations drift, they guide the group back to focus. They normalize transparency, naming constraints, uncertainties, risks, and assumptions to support healthier participation. They understand that presence without purpose drains energy, and they respect when people say no to a meeting for the right reasons.

These behaviors create psychological safety not because they are soft, but because they are steady. People trust leaders who communicate with clarity.

CHAPTER 12 REFLECTION

Use these questions to deepen your thinking before you move on:

- What behaviors do I model in meetings, intentionally or unintentionally?

- Where might my team be mirroring a lack of clarity that I didn't realize I was signaling?

- How can I use CLEAR language consistently, so others feel confident doing the same?

- Which leadership moment this week is the strongest opportunity to model clarity?

CONCLUSION

You began this book by stepping into a familiar frustration—the meetings that drain energy, stall progress, and quietly teach people to expect less from one another. You've seen the cost of unclear expectations, unfocused conversations, and gatherings that happen out of habit rather than intention. But now you also know something equally true: meetings aren't the problem. The way we design them is.

Meetings are the heartbeat of how we communicate, collaborate, and lead. They shape culture in real time. And when they are clear, intentional, and designed with relevance in mind, everything else gets easier. Decisions sharpen. Alignment strengthens. Teams trust more. The work flows.

You don't need a sweeping transformation to get there. You don't need permission. You don't need more time or bigger teams. You need one thing: the willingness to stop accepting the meeting culture you inherited and start creating the one you want.

I've watched leaders use CLEAR to shift not only their meetings but their entire way of working. Their conversations became focused on value. Their teams grew more confident. Their calendars felt lighter because the meetings they kept finally mattered. Clarity creates momentum quickly; once people feel it, they don't want to go back.

And this is your moment to choose differently.

You don't have to tolerate agendas that drift, attendance that feels obligatory, or conversations that leave everyone wondering what actually happened. You don't have to roll your eyes at yet another meeting invite. You can break the cycle that has been normalized for far too long. The change begins with one meeting you decide to make CLEAR. Then another. And another. That's how meeting culture shifts, quietly at first, then undeniably.

This is how meetings get reimagined. This is how teams rediscover energy. This is how leaders save time, build trust, and create real progress. And if enough of us do it, this is how we save the world, one meeting at a time.

You already have everything you need. Why wait? Choose clarity today. Choose intention today. Today, choose meetings that move your work forward, not just through your calendar.

Now, repeat after me…

You have nothing to fear when the meeting is CLEAR.

PART IV

TEMPLATES

Knowing CLEAR is powerful. Using it is transformative. Part IV offers simple, ready-to-apply tools and templates that bring the framework to life. These resources make it easier to design, run, and reflect on meetings with confidence and intention.

Template #1: The CLEAR Canvas

The CLEAR Canvas

OUTCOMES (what success looks like: verb + objective + context)	ENGAGE THE ESSENTIAL PEOPLE (who must attend)
1 _____	_____
2 _____	_____
3 _____	_____

PURPOSE
(why we're meeting: action + focus + why now)

_____

ROLES & EXPECTATIONS (how they will participate)	RELEVANCE (why it matters to them)
Facilitator: _____	You will _____
Contributors _____ _____	This helps you _____
Challenger(s) _____	Your perspective matters because _____

A CLEAR meeting is a meeting worth having.

Template #2: Should This Be a Meeting?

SHOULD THIS BE A MEETING?

A quick check to see if this meeting is ready.

(1) Can you state the purpose in a concise sentence?

☐ Yes

☐ No. If the why is missing, the meeting should be too.

(2) Do you know what must be created, decided, or clarified by the end?

☐ Yes

☐ No. If the outcome isn't clear, the meeting won't be either.

(3) Do you know who is essential, and why?

☐ Yes

☐ No. If everyone is invited, no one is accountable.

(4) Do you know how each person needs to contribute?

☐ Yes

☐ No. Unclear roles guarantee confusion.

(5) Can you articulate why this meeting matters to them?

☐ Yes

☐ No. If it doesn't matter to them, their attention won't either.

If any answer above is "No," the meeting is not ready. Before scheduling, make it CLEAR. Consider if asynchronous could work.
A CLEAR meeting is a meeting worth having.

Template #3: Outcome-Based Agenda

OUTCOME-BASED AGENDA

A CLEAR meeting is a meeting worth having.

Purpose: *action + focus + why now*

Outcomes: *verb + objective + context*
1.
2.
3.

Timebox	Facilitator or Lead	Agenda Item (Link to Outcomes)	Format (Group discussion, silent brainstorm, voting, etc)
5 min	Facilitator	Set the Frame	Name the Purpose, Outcomes, and Roles
10 min	Facilitator	Summarize	Name Decisions Made, Action Items + Owners, Next Steps

Template #4: Meeting Reflection Note Card

MEETING REFLECTION

Reflect and adapt so your meetings evolve instead of repeat

What worked?

What helped us?
What moved us forward?

What didn't work?

What slowed us down?
What got in the way?

What will we try next time?

REFERENCES

Atlassian. "Workplace Woes: Meetings Edition." *Work Life* (blog). Accessed December 9, 2025. https://www.atlassian. com/blog/workplace-woes-meetings

Reclaim.ai. *Microsoft Outlook Productivity Trends Report. Reclaim.ai* (blog). May 12, 2025. https://reclaim.ai/blog/ microsoft-outlook-productivity-report

Microsoft. *Work Trend Index Special Report: Breaking Down the Infinite Workday. WorkLab* (blog). June 17, 2025. https:// www.microsoft.com/en-us/worklab/work-trend-index/ breaking-down-infinite-workday